I Desire Mercy…

a transformation of the heart

Minister Ehlei Chandler

Contact Information

Email: ministere1@yahoo.com
Myspace: myspace.com/ministere1

ISBN: 978-1-60383-107-9

Published by:
Holy Fire Publishing
717 Old Trolley Road
Attn: Suite 116, Publishing Unit #116
Summerville, SC 29485

www.ChristianPublish.com

Printed in the United States of America and the United Kingdom

ACKNOWLEDGEMENTS

JESUS CHRIST

HE is GOD manifested in the flesh, HE lived a perfect and sinless life, and HE was beaten, crucified, and died for the sins of all humanity. Three days later, arose from the dead, showed HIMSELF alive, and ascended to HIS place in honor, glory, and authority in heaven. And, one day HE is returning to take HIS people out of this world, to dwell with HIM forever. AMEN. I love you LORD.

My Wife

You are a true woman of GOD, helper, and friend. Thank you baby.

Pastor Rackley

Who has helped me find out, accept, and become who I am. I appreciate you.

My mom, thanks for everything. My entire Mighty Fortress of GOD family. In addition, much love to all who are the true body of CHRIST. I LOVE YOU ALL.

Table of Contents

PREFACE

Hosea 6:6 For I desire mercy and not sacrifice, and the knowledge of GOD more than burnt offerings.

GOD has always delighted in heartfelt loyalty to HIS blood covenant, instead of empty pious acts associated with tradition, religion, and legalism. Moreover, HE wants us to know HIM truly, rather than just giving and doing physical things that do not benefit a spiritual GOD.

This is not to say we are not to give offerings and sacrifice to GOD, but rather go back to find or remember the purpose. Piety is great, when performed through a heart that is sold out. When we understand that it's not for GODs benefit, but ours, that we would grow in grace and become selfless in all aspects of life.

This book is for everyone, for non-Christians to learn the truth of who, and how, we are. For new Christians, this can be a tool for learning how to serve GOD. It can also be used to rekindle the fire in those who have been in this thing for a while, and may have become stagnant or tired in the battle. And to those who are bound in secret sin, unable to break free, this will show you how to walk in true deliverance through the SPIRIT of GOD. In addition, I pray all who read this begin to move in a little closer to our wonderful savior, JESUS CHRIST.

I pray this book will be a blessing to your life, as writing it has been a blessing to mine.

GRACE AND PEACE

INTRODUCTION

Our daily lives should never become routine in our service to GOD, knowing HE can at any time and in any way, meet us where we are. Mt. Sinai was not the promised land, but Moses and the children of Israel could have stayed there, just because GOD met them there. However, serving GOD means looking past what we think seems right and waiting for HIM to speak, guide, and lead. We sometimes feel that we should stop, and stay, in the first place we experience GOD. But that is where tradition and religion starts, doing the same thing tomorrow that we did today; causing a pattern of doing things without prayer and forfeiting the ability and desire to hear GODs voice again. Why seek and pray? We know what HE wants, HE spoke already; we have HIS plan all figured out. This is how GOD is taken out of the equation and religion is born.

Exodus 40:36-38 this scripture is paramount in living for CHRIST, because it shows us how to follow the leader (pastor) GOD places in our lives, and teaches us to trust GOD for ourselves. Exodus 20:18-19 reminds us how we are in the beginning of our walk with

CHRIST, needing someone to almost carry us in every way, spiritually; not being able to hear or understand GODs voice, but having GODs man or woman speak for HIM. They are here for the perfecting of the church, and with time and obedience, we can be the next one GOD uses to continue the perfecting.

Then, here in 40:36-38 the cloud and glory filling the tabernacle represents the HOLY SPIRIT filling us, and when HE moves, we move. If we are filled and can discern the in the spirit, we will notice when the anointing is not in what we are doing, beginning to follow the anointing where it goes. It starts with Proverbs 3:5-6 and ends with Galatians 5:16.

True service to GOD will, if nothing else, keep us on our toes. Yes the bible says HE is the same GOD yesterday, today, and forever; but we've got to find out who HE is and what HE does before we can assume to know HIS plan for us, or how HE will deal with us today.

Pious acts, outside of fellowship with GOD, are dead. HE knows how to, and will, lead us in what pleases HIM. If the heart of GOD is not in what we do, what is it done for? If it's not ordained by GOD, why do it? One reason is, just as the Pharisees, we want to be seen and thought of as highly spiritual. Even when struggling, we can put up the front that everything is all right, instead of dropping piety and asking for help. What we need to do is stop walking in pride, and serve GOD regardless of circumstance or consequence. The steps of the righteous man are ordered by GOD: and he is happy in his way. Psalm 37:23. That means, serve GOD for the purpose of your soul, not the purpose of pleasing men, and you will be joyful.

Without faith, it is impossible to please GOD. Hebrews 11:6. Therefore, all the works don't please HIM; but it's the heart that is led by faith and guidance to do those works, to justify our faith, that pleases GOD. We have only one tradition to keep, which is going to the LORD, to find out HIS plan for us daily. Proverbs 3:5-6 and Matthew 7:7-8. Keep asking, seeking, and knocking until HE speaks. Here's the thing, if we are sent by GOD, HE will give provision and we cannot fail in that endeavor, because it's HIS plan. But when we plan out our own lives; doing it our way, with no regard for GODs timing or purpose, we miss the steps that must be taken and either fall into a snare or grow weary of walking in our own strength. If the steps we take are nor ordained, the anointing will not flow in that area, resulting in having no strength from GOD. Isaiah 40:31 says but they that wait on the LORD shall renew their strength; they shall mount up with wings as eagles; they shall run, and not be weary; they shall walk, and not faint. Do it GODs way and you don't have to get tired.

Psalm 37:23 does not mean whatever we so is ordered, but when we have died to ourselves, we'll be in a place we are ready to be led; and those who are led of the SPIRIT of GOD, they are the sons of GOD. For of we do these things ourselves, GOD does not get glory.

Mercy comes from a heart that has been renewed by GOD. Our hearts must be conformed to GODs heart, and our minds to GODs mind.

1 Samuel 15:22; obedience is better than sacrifice. Doing what GOD called us to do is better than doing things that seem holy, without instruction from LORD. Everything we do or desire to do must be filtered through the SPIRIT of GOD. HIS kingdom come, HIS will be done.

WALKING BY FAITH

Hebrews 11:1-2 Now faith is the substance of things hoped for, the evidence of things not seen. For by it the elders obtained a good report.

With faith, we should not be affected by sight, but what we see should always be affected by faith. Faith is holding on to what is true, what GOD means for our lives; knowing, all things work together for good to them that love GOD, and are called according to HIS purpose (Romans 8:28). Those who have mature faith don't trust appearance; they trust the WORD, which is the very heart of GOD. That's why without faith it is impossible to please HIM, faith trusts GOD when we would waver. Faith will begin to alter the perception of what we see to what GOD knows. Faith comes by hearing, but we must hear the WORD of GOD.

When we worry and complain about things we cannot change, we show our lack of trust in GOD. This means we are walking according to the flesh at those moments, or we really don't believe GOD can, and will, make a way out of no way, and we don't think HE will do what HE said HE will do.

When we worry and complain about things we can change, we take away our own ability to grow; because we sit on our back sides, refusing to do what needs to be done, what GOD has already empowered us to do.

We as Christians must overcome the human instinct to fail, worry, and complain; and it will not happen without the SPIRIT of GOD dwelling in us. Once this is achieved, we will no longer live frustrated and defeated lives. But we can't walk in the flesh and overcome the enemy. If life and death are in the power of the tongue, but there is no life (SPIRIT of GOD) in us, then that power is not manifested in us, we cannot speak life. We have to first learn to "submit to GOD and resist the devil" before he will flee, James 4:7. That is when GOD can trust us, and impart in us HIS power and authority; that's the anointing on our lives. Without that power, we can't speak a word, lay hands on the sick (so they recover), cast out demons, and take dominion in the spirit or in our lives. Galatians

5:16 says, walk in the spirit and you will not fulfill the lust of the flesh. First, to walk in the spirit means to stop living to please ourselves, change the obvious contradictions between us and the WORD (through fasting and prayer), and listen to the conviction from the HOLY SPIRIT. In addition, we have to stay accountable to someone who is spiritually mature i.e. pastors, ministers, and spiritual fathers and mothers. Do these things and get busy in the ministry, and I guarantee you will see exponential growth in your life. As many as are led of the SPIRIT of GOD, they are the sons of GOD, Romans 8:14. Child of GOD, allow yourself to receive of HIS abundance of blessings and joy in all aspects of your life. Amen.

Now that we have covered what faith is, let's talk about the bible as a weapon of warfare.

2Timothy 3:16-17: all scripture is given by inspiration of GOD, and is profitable for doctrine, for reproof, for correction, for instruction in righteousness: that the man of GOD may be perfect, thoroughly furnished (equipped for) all works. Keep knowledge of the fact that the bible is real, not just sayings or stories of fiction. Know in your heart that this is a book from GOD to you. So you do not have to wonder if you can receive from the WORD, it is yours already. Matthew 9:29: JESUS says, "according to your faith, be it unto you. Your belief in the WORD will cause it to manifest in the physical.

Isaiah 54:17 no weapon formed against you shall prosper. Let this be a foundation set in you heart and mind. The weapon will be formed and it will be used against you, but it will not fulfill Satan's purpose to harm you. Therefore, when things seem to fall apart in your life, stop crying and fight. The outcome will always be in your favor, if you only believe. And, count it all joy, James 1:2-3 says when you are tried and troubled, it only makes you stronger.

Now, here is some ammo for the battle.

Battling sickness:

Exodus 15:26 If thou wilt diligently hearken to the voice of the LORD thy God, and wilt do that which is right in his sight, and wilt give ear to his commandments, and keep all his statutes, I will put none of these diseases upon thee, which I have brought upon the Egyptians: for I [am] the LORD that healeth thee. When we truly live holy, to please GOD, HE will truly have your back. Read 2 Kings 20:1-5, GOD proved it to Hezekiah.

Jeremiah 30:17 For I will restore health unto thee, and I will heal thee of thy wounds, saith the LORD; because they called thee an Outcast, [saying], This [is] Zion, whom no man seeketh after. Just to show unbelievers HE is not mocked, to show that Christians are not alone and crazy, GOD will display HIS power through your healing.

James 5:14-15 Is any sick among you? let him call for the elders of the church; and let them pray over him, anointing him with oil in the name of the Lord: And the prayer of faith shall save the sick, and the Lord shall raise him up; and if he have committed sins, they shall be forgiven him. Just another reason we need to be in a church home. Altogether, GOD is able and your healing is in HIS hands.

For the discontent and weak:

Philippians 4:6-8 Be careful for nothing; but in every thing by prayer and supplication with thanksgiving let your requests be made known unto God. And the peace of God, which passeth all understanding, shall keep your hearts and minds through Christ Jesus.

Finally, brethren, whatsoever things are true, whatsoever things [are] honest, whatsoever things [are] just, whatsoever things [are] pure, whatsoever things [are] lovely, whatsoever things [are] of good report; if [there be] any virtue, and if [there be] any praise, think on these things. If you don't worry about things, but pray about all things, leave them in GODs hands, and keep your mind on good and peaceful things, you will be content and have peace no matter what is going on in your life.

1Timothy 6:6 But godliness with contentment is great gain. This is not to say, sit and do nothing, but your desire for more should not cause frustration or worry, if you never get more. What of GOD calls you to be like John the Baptist, who lived in the wilderness but prepared the way of the LORD? Remember, GOD is sovereign and knows what's best. In all things do your best to let GOD lead you.

Ephesians 3:16 That he would grant you, according to the riches of his glory, to be strengthened with might by his Spirit in the inner man. GOD will do it, but you've got to believe and walk by faith in it.

Philippians 4:13 I can do all things through Christ which strengtheneth me. All the questions you may have, like, can I, or should I go back to school, college, get a better job, start a business, etc. You can take a step of faith, knowing that the fasting and praying has caused you to become sensitive enough to know GODs timing. Things are easier when we follow the anointing, do it HIS way. GOD allows our desires to come to pass, if they lead us to a place HE gets glory.

2Corinthians 10:4-5 For the weapons of our warfare [are] not carnal, but mighty through God to the pulling down of strong holds, Casting down imaginations, and every high thing that exalteth itself against the knowledge of God, and bringing into captivity every thought to the obedience of Christ. There is nothing weak about you or the one you serve, and what GOD has given you is far greater than anything the enemy, the world, or the flesh can throw at you. Stand and fight, for you are to be strong in the LORD and in the power of HIS might, don't walk by your strength, walk in GODs.

Struggling with fear:

1John 4:18 There is no fear in love; but perfect love casteth out fear: because fear hath torment. He that feareth is not made perfect in love.

Fear is from the enemy, and when we realize GODs love for us is so great; that HE will not let Satan do whatever he wants in our lives. We can be at peace, knowing the trials and tribulation are structured by GOD to make us better. Even though it may hurt, there should be no fear in being perfected.

John 10:28 And I give unto them eternal life; and they shall never perish, neither shall any [man] pluck them out of my hand. Yes, we live in a fallen world, and evil is all around us, but GOD is able to keep us safe and protected. Psalm 91:10 says no evil shall befall you, nor shall any plague come near your dwelling. Just be in CHRIST and trust HIM, everything WILL BE all right. Also, 1Peter 5:10 says but the GOD of all grace, who called us to HIS eternal glory by CHRIST JESUS, after you have suffered a while, perfect you, established you, strengthen you, and settle you. So, don't get weary while you're in the oven, when you come out, you will be as pure gold.

No longer a slave to sin:

Read Romans chapter 7. Once we receive CHRIST, we realize how hard it is to say no to the flesh, which has been ruling so long. We realize the hunger, now that we are trying to starve the old nature and feed the new man. Paul said whenever I want to do right; I inevitably do what is wrong. When you hear that from the greatest apostle, it can be unnerving; he had trouble saying no to himself, fleshly desire was still overwhelming.

However, thank GOD that's not the final result of being a Christian.

Now read Romans chapter 8. There is no more condemnation for sin, but repentance, forgiveness, and deliverance lie in wait for those who serve GOD. Meditation, prayer, fasting, and time are the cure for sins grasp on our life. One of my favorite scriptures, Galatians 5:16 says walk in the spirit, and you will not fulfill the lust of the flesh, you have to exercise your spirit before you can overcome. Keep fighting, and after a while, you will keep winning.

FASTING AND PRAYING

Ezra 8:23 So we fasted and earnestly prayed that our God would take care of us, and he heard our prayer. (NLT)

What is fasting?

A fast is when you give up food to get closer to GOD, to exercise faith, to push past the hindrance of answered prayer. However, without fervent prayer during the abstinence of food, it's just a diet. It's as if you are giving up physical food for spiritual food, in order to complete a task, that otherwise could not be done. You should fast when you cannot hear GOD, need guidance, getting entangled in the ways of the world, when your flesh seems to be stronger than your spirit, when you feel oppressed, and when you are facing war or death.

Isaiah 58:6-12

The kind of fasting I want calls you to free those who are wrongly imprisoned and to stop oppressing those who work for you. Treat them fairly and give them what they earn. I want you to share your food with the hungry and to welcome poor wanderers into your homes. Give clothes to those who need them, and do not hide from relatives who need your help.

"If you do these things, your salvation will come like the dawn. Yes, your healing will come quickly. Your godliness will lead you forward, and the glory of the Lord will protect you from behind. Then when you call, the Lord will answer. `Yes, I am here,' he will quickly reply.

"Stop oppressing the helpless and stop making false accusations and spreading vicious rumors! Feed the hungry and help those in trouble. Then your light will shine out from the darkness, and the darkness around you will be as bright as day. The Lord will guide you continually, watering your life when you are dry and keeping you healthy, too. You will be like a well-watered garden, like an ever-flowing spring. Your children will rebuild the deserted ruins of your cities. Then you will be known as the people who rebuild their walls and cities. (NLT)

This is a clear outline of the reason for fasting. Now, as for how long the fast should be, and what to give up (this is to those who have physical ailments, who cannot abstain from food. You can abstain from tv, movies, video games, even friends; for a time, to give yourself more completely to GOD in prayer.) is between you and GOD.

However, we should never fast for selfish and prideful ambition. 1 Samuel 14:24 and the men of Israel were distressed that day, for Saul had placed the people under oath, saying, cursed is the man who eats any food until evening, before I have taken vengeance on my enemies. So none of the people tasted food. Saul did not pray and ask GOD for victory, he did not fast so GOD would intervene, or that GOD would be glorified; he did not want anyone to eat until he got glory in battle.

However, here is a basic outline for differing lengths and types of fasts.

There is the one day fast, usually during a battle, which is a petition to GOD for HIS divine victory. During this day, set aside for prayer and warfare, you should eat nothing until sundown. 2 Chronicles 20:3-4 and Jehoshaphat feared, and set himself to seek the LORD, and proclaimed a fast throughout all Judah. So Judah gathered together to ask help from the LORD; and from all the cities of Judah they came to seek the LORD.

Judges 20:26 Then all the children of Israel, and all the people, went up, and came unto the house of God, and wept, and sat there before the LORD, and fasted that day until even, and offered burnt offerings and peace offerings before the LORD.

Since the battle does not pause, there may be no time to fast for a long time; so, sometimes you need something quick and to the point.

The three day fast, no food or drink, has been used for overwhelmingly heavy burdens. With nothing else going on but prayer and supplication. This says to GOD, I need your help more than anything else; no work, no play, and no friends, just fast and pray. Read Esther chapter 4.

Seven day fasts are, in the bible, done mostly for mourning. 1Samuel 31:13 says And they took their bones, and buried [them] under a tree at Jabesh, and fasted seven days.

Though it does not have to be mourning the loss of someone, but maybe for a frustrated and depressed life; looking to GOD to restore joy and wholeness to a life that has been broken.

Twenty-one day fast. (Daniel 10:3) Daniel was mourning because of his lack of understanding; he did not know what his vision meant. He put his flesh lower to get clarity from GOD. You may want to hear GOD's voice clearer in your everyday walk, or need clarity on GODs purpose for your life; whatever the purpose, anything up to twenty-one days will get it done. The fact of the matter is I was on a twenty-one day fast when I was led to write this book. The church I attend does a twenty-one day fast at least once a year, usually in January, to get guidance for that year. And GOD does not have to take long at all; HE began to deal with me about this book on the fourth day of the fast. HE will come through for you, just watch.

The forty-day fast seems to be strictly for the start of a ministry. JESUS and Moses did this one, and when we look at what their lives produced, we can see why it was necessary. Moses had the weight of a nation (their needs, complaints, and sins) on his shoulders. His flesh, in the spiritual sense, had to die. Imagine being the voice for GOD among the people, you got to be sure not to get it wrong. JESUS had the weight of the world on HIS shoulders, and it was not easy. Matthew 26:38-39 Then saith he unto them, My soul is exceeding sorrowful, even unto death: tarry ye here, and watch with me. And he went a little further, and fell on his face, and prayed, saying, O my Father, if it be possible, let this cup pass from me: nevertheless not as I will, but as thou [wilt]. The forty-day fast could be the difference between submitting to death and preserving your own life.

What it's like to fast, any length of time.

First, everyone has to walk in wisdom and guidance of the HOLY SPIRIT, knowing what they are getting themselves into, before going in. Fasting puts our flesh under subjection to the SPIRIT OF GOD, and it is a sacrifice; but we should not feel like we are really dying, or unable to function in our everyday life. We obviously get hunger pangs, but if JESUS says do not appear to fast unto men, then HE will give us the ability to do so. The physical hardships that come from fasting are natural, but if it is so overwhelming that you cannot work through it on the job or in public, then you should eat unless you have time off, and can commit to pushing past the pain. Some things that I have encountered when fasting are dizziness, headaches, and extreme fatigue; and I have found it is better to eat than hurt yourself.

When fasting, you must be willing to submit to GODs will. If a fast does not begin to make you malleable, to be molded by GOD, either the SPIRIT OF GOD is not in it or your heart is not in it, meaning you could be wasting your time. Something we must remember is, just doing things that are considered right is not what blesses us. Even JESUS was led by the SPIRIT into the wilderness to start HIS fast, therefore, ordained for that time.

Fast from the things of life but don't fast from life itself, don't walk around like a zombie because you cannot eat, sleep with your spouse, play video games, and go to the movies; you still have brothers and sisters to fellowship with, pray with, and sharpen your sword with. Help build one another up in the things of GOD, that way the fast doesn't have to seem so hard.

When fasting, go back to basics with Philippians 4:6-9, because thinking about not eating is the hardest part of a fast; instead, think about what you are fasting for, why the fast is important, and why you should continue.

Prior to and during a fast, all types of things will begin to happen; such as, everyone wants to invite you out to eat, throwing parties, or just eating tempting food all in your face. Your enemy will always do all it takes to deter you from overcoming, and that means causing you to break every fast; he knows the benefit of turning down your plate, and what you will be able to do to him and his kingdom. Just know that you will never be patient if your faith is not tried.

Still, a fast is not a fast without prayer, and those prayers must be continual. The continual prayer keeps your mind off food, keeps the pressure off you, and keeps the pressure on Satan; it makes him stay on the defensive, he cannot attack you while you are attacking him. Our victory, our power, our deliverance, our healing, and our sanity is in prayer; the only difference is that fasting takes the potency of prayer to the next level.

Matthew 6:9-13 is a model of prayer from JESUS himself, it is not meant to be prayed verbatim, but you should fashion your prayers after this. Here is a slightly clearer understanding of the model.

Our FATHER in heaven denotes the direction of prayer, recognition of power and authority, and it shows we know HE is the source.

Hallowed be your name. Hallowed means holy, set apart, and revered. Name signifies character and authority if GOD. We are coming before HIM, glorifying HIM, reverencing HIM, and believing HIM because of who HE is. This is praise and worship.

Your kingdom come, Your will be done on earth, as it is in heaven. Through my praise, worship, and reverence to you LORD; give me your will, your desire, your purpose for my life. What you have established in heaven, establish here on earth, through me; I am willing to submit to you and die to myself.

Give us this day our daily bread. As you reveal your will to me, provide what I need to fulfill it. You are the source and I am in need, everything you have, I want.

Forgive our debts as we forgive our debtors. Repenting and forgiving, 1 Corinthians 13:5 love does not keep an account of wrong that has been done to it, and 1 John 1:9, if we confess our sins, HE is faithful and just to forgive us our sins, and to cleanse us from all unrighteousness.

Lead us not into temptation. Don't allow us to be overtaken in our flesh, or led away by our own lust; James 1:14 says but every man is tempted, when he is drawn away of his own lust, and enticed. LORD, keep us from that old way of thinking and change our instincts.

But deliver us from the evil one. Give us your power to overcome. Put your super on our natural. Raise up a standard and provide the victory. Psalms 25:2 O my GOD, I trust in the: let me not be ashamed, let not my enemies triumph over me. Isaiah 59:19b when the enemy shall come in like a flood, the SPIRIT of the LORD shall lift up a standard against him.

For yours is the kingdom, the power, and the glory forever. Amen. Praise and worship again, for all HE is doing and is about to do; because it is truly done by HIM. AMEN.

CHURCH

Why do I have to go to church?

Hebrews 10:24-25 And let us consider one another to provoke unto love and to good works: Not forsaking the assembling of ourselves together, as the manner of some [is]; but exhorting [one another]: and so much the more, as ye see the day approaching.

In Greek it sounds more like this: and we must understand one another, and how to cause love and good works to be manifested, do not ever abandon the physical gathering of ourselves, as the custom of some; but persuade, admonish, and comfort: and much more, as you see the day approaching.

When we exegete this scripture, we find it is a command and not a suggestion. So, while many say they don't need to go to church to be saved, we see through the light of the word that we cannot live in obedience disobeying commands. Also, Ephesians 4:11-13 begs the question, how do those not in church become all they can in CHRIST? And most people who don't want to go to church don't want to be accountable, to their lack of growth, and still desire to please themselves. Those who desire to go to church realize their need for a leader that will push them harder than they will themselves, and they know that being in ministry is paramount to GOD using them.

There are also those who don't want to go to church, because they think all pastors are stealing money. First, do they really believe no ones is living holy? GOD has a covenant people, doing what HE called them to do. And to make things clear, tithe and offering is for the benefit of the one that gives: Luke 6:38. Let GOD deal with the thieves, you find a church home and be blessed by giving.

There are two definitions for assembly in the Greek, ekklesia, which is the one used for church everywhere in the New Testament, is not a physical building, but the body of believers. Episynagoge is the one used in Hebrews, and means physical gathering in one place.

What a leader is.

Now that you know why go to church, this is who should be your leader.

Romans 10:14 how then shall they call on HIM in whom they have not believed? And haw shall they believe in HIM of whom they have not heard? And how shall hear without a preacher? That preacher has to be a kainos anthropos (new man) 1 Samuel 10:6, and must be sent by GOD.

Ephesians 4:11-13 and HE gave some, apostles; and some, prophets; and some, evangelists; and some, pastors and teachers; for the perfecting of the saints, for the work of the ministry, for the edifying of the body of CHRIST: till we all come in the unity of the faith, and of the knowledge of the SON of GOD, unto a perfect man, unto the measure of the stature of the fullness of CHRIST. GOD puts people in your life that are where you need to be, to raise you up and perfect you for ministry.

1 Timothy 3:1-7. Verse 6 says not a novice, lest being lifted up with pride he fall into the condemnation of the devil. He can't be a beginner with no record of sound doctrine.

1 Timothy 5:17 let the elders that rule well be counted worthy of double honor, especially they who labor in the word and doctrine. If the pastor has a love for the labor in word and doctrine, if he teaches truth without fear of people turning away; if you see the burden of love for those ho is serving, take care of that person in every way you can, and GOD will take care of you.

Purpose for every ministry

Though pastors have a very important job, they are not the only ones. Every person that joins a ministry is vital; I'm not talking about joining a church to warm a seat, but those who join because they believe in the vision of the church and want to help bring it to pass. Everyone has been given a gift by GOD, and that gift is to be used for GOD's glory to touch a heart, mind, or spirit. The anointing can flow through many avenues, which causes yokes to be destroyed, chains to be broken, and burdens to be removed; the need for these blessings in the anointing shows that pastors need you just as much as you need pastors.

1Corinthians 12:5-11 There are different kinds of service in the church, but it is the same Lord we are serving. There are different ways God works in our lives, but it is the same God who does the work through all of us. A spiritual gift is given to each of us as a means of helping the entire church. To one person the Spirit gives the ability to give wise advice; to another he gives the gift of special knowledge. The Spirit gives special faith to another, and to someone else he gives the power to heal the sick. He gives one person the power to perform miracles, and to another the ability to prophesy. He gives someone else the ability to know whether it is really the Spirit of God or another spirit that is speaking. Still another person is given the ability to speak in unknown languages, and another is given the ability to interpret what is being said. It is the one and only Holy Spirit who distributes these gifts. He alone decides which gift each person should have. (NLT)

To go a step further, singing, dancing, ushering, guidance, street ministry, just being able to show the love of GOD to everyone, etc; these will all be used to perfect the body of CHRIST on earth. However, if our reason for doing any of this is not to bless someone or bring someone to the knowledge of the glory of GOD, then it is being done in vain. Again, it's not enough to join a ministry because your friends did, it may be fun to do, or because you want to be seen; you must learn to maximize your potential in GOD, through the perfecting of your gifts. PLEASE REMEMBER, THE CHURCH NEEDS YOUR SPIRITUAL GIFTS.

Giving

2 Corinthians 9:6-15 Remember this-a farmer who plants only a few seeds will get a small crop. But the one who plants generously will get a generous crop. You must each make up your own mind as to how much you should give. Don't give reluctantly or in response to pressure. For God loves the person who gives cheerfully. And God will generously provide all you need. Then you will always have everything you need and plenty left over to share with others. As the Scriptures say,

"Godly people give generously to the poor.

Their good deeds will never be forgotten."

For God is the one who gives seed to the farmer and then bread to eat. In the same way, he will give you many opportunities to do good, and he will produce a great harvest of generosity in you.

Yes, you will be enriched so that you can give even more generously. And when we take your gifts to those who need them, they will break out in thanksgiving to God. So two good things will happen-the needs of the Christians in Jerusalem will be met, and they will joyfully express their thanksgiving to God. You will be glorifying God through your generous gifts. For your generosity to them will prove that you are obedient to the Good News of Christ. And they will pray for you with deep affection because of the wonderful grace of God shown through you.

Thank God for his Son-- gift too wonderful for words! (NLT)

It must first be understood that giving is of GOD, John 3:16 GOD so loved… HE gave;

love is giving and GOD is love, if GOD is in us then we must give. 2 Cor. 9:6-15 is just an outline of what we should be doing; it shows the purpose for tithes and offerings and what the church should be using them for. Also, this scripture, in addition to Acts 4:34-35 are just fulfillment of the prophecy in Malachi 3:1-12; yes, I said prophecy, future tense and the fulfillment is to continue forever.

Here is what JESUS said in Matthew 10:40-42 "He who receives you receives Me, and he who receives Me receives Him who sent Me. He who receives a prophet in the name of a prophet shall receive a prophet's reward. And he who receives a righteous man in the name of a righteous man shall receive a righteous man's reward. And whoever gives one of these little ones only a cup of cold water in the name of a disciple, assuredly, I say to you, he shall by no means lose his reward."

Everyone JESUS named is a leader in HIS house, and as you give into that person or house, as they give into your life, you fulfill GODs will to give.

It gets deeper. The separation of certain verses of scripture causes a misunderstanding of the meaning. Take for instance, Galatians 6:6 is always preached separate from verses 7-10, but GOD showed me something while I was studying.

Galatians 6:7 says do not be led astray, GOD will not be jeered or laughed at, as if what HE says will not come to pass; whatever you put into the ground of life, that is what you will harvest. When preached separately, that scripture could almost stand alone, but there is an explanation in the context (surrounding text); then even more scripture is used to make the apologia, which means a case or defense for a belief or theory.

Here it is: Galatians 6:6 says let him who is taught in the word share in all good things with him who teaches. Going to Deuteronomy 33:10, Levi was the teacher of GODs people, Joshua 13:14, Levi was the only tribe not to get an inheritance; but would receive from each tribe a portion of their inheritance. JESUS continued this "trend" if you will, in Luke 9:3-5. The disciples were sent out to teach about the kingdom of GOD, and were told not to take anything along; they were to be housed, clothed, fed, and provided for in every way by those they taught. This is backed up in Matthew 10:40-42, receive them and give them even a cup of water, and receive GOD and HIS blessings; but not just water, share in all good things, whatever you sow, you will reap.

To make it clear, from Malachi 3:8-10, tithe is for the storehouse and is used to keep the house of GOD running and to help those in need. Offerings are for the overseer of GODs house, that they will be taken care of while they take care of you. 1 Corinthians 9:11-14 If we have sown spiritual things for you, is it a great thing if we reap your material things? If others are partakers of this right over you, are we not even more?

Nevertheless we have not used this right, but endure all things lest we hinder the gospel of Christ. Do you not know that those who minister the holy things eat of the things of the temple, and those who serve at the altar partake of the offerings of the altar? Even so the Lord has commanded that those who preach the gospel should live from the gospel. Paul called it their right, meaning it was supposed to be practiced, but wasn't. Tithes and offerings are a staple for keeping all GODs people blessed.

MARRIAGE

Genesis 2:18 And the LORD God said, [It is] not good that the man should be alone; I will make him an help meet for him.

Purpose for marriage.

Prior to sexism, feminism, pride from making more money, and the plain old me, myself, and I attitude; it was and is GODs plan for a woman to be the helper of a man. Adam and Eve were joined in a perfect union by GOD, no question of "am I sure this is the one?"; the question that has come up ever since people have become all about self. Men have become driven by sight, choosing rather to find the best-looking woman than to find the woman who best meets the need in his life. Women have decided to be the leader instead of the helper, and calls GODs man less of a man if he does not do all she requires. If we as the body of CHRIST will learn our role in CHRIST, we would not have such a hard time finding a spouse; but, that not being the case, we must go through premarital counseling in order to better learn who that really is that you are with. There are many things that are not found out about the other person because we would rather believe "loving" that person is enough, than to talk about those tough subjects; premarital counseling will bring the truth out, like it or not.

Let us look at the original purpose for a helper. All the work that was placed in Adams care, Eve was to help accomplish. Someone who could meet Adam on his level, someone to converse, laugh, love, work, and procreate with. Notice that physical abuse, someone to blame for hardships, or have as a slave is not mentioned. It is for oneness and sharing, not selfishness; for overcoming together, not pointing the finger to feel better or get out of trouble. Sin brought all those things about, and with counseling, we can stave off the effects, through teaching and prayer. We can and must go back to the original and still current plan of GOD; we have to take on those characteristics before saying "I do".

1 Corinthians 7:1-3 Now concerning the things whereof ye wrote unto me: [It is] good for a man not to touch a woman. Nevertheless, [to

avoid] fornication, let every man have his own wife, and let every woman have her own husband. Let the husband render unto the wife due benevolence: and likewise also the wife unto the husband. Respect and love are two separate entities, and must be dealt with as such. Men deal with relationships through respect and women deal with them through love. Most men do not know how to love a woman the way she needs to be loved, in order to see what she should respect in him. Most women do not know how to respect and submit to a man in the way that will open the door inside him for love to flow.

We will come back to verse 4 later.

One thing that is breaking up so many marriages is lack of love and lack of submission; which is dealt with in Ephesians 5:22-33.

Verses 22-24: Wives, submit yourselves unto your own husbands, as unto the Lord. For the husband is the head of the wife, even as Christ is the head of the church: and he is the savior of the body. Therefore as the church is subject unto Christ, so [let] the wives [be] to their own husbands in every thing.

This clearly means, the way you serve CHRIST; in obedience, reverence, care, and humility, you should likewise serve your husband. Understand that the way wives carry on in their marriage mirrors their love for GOD, if you cannot submit to your husband, how can you submit to GOD? And vise versa. Women, don't even contemplate marriage until this scripture is accepted and settled in your mind, body, and spirit.

Verses 25-31: Husbands, love your wives, even as Christ also loved the church, and gave himself for it; That he might sanctify and cleanse it with the washing of water by the word, That he might present it to himself a glorious church, not having spot, or wrinkle, or any such thing; but that it should be holy and without blemish. So ought men to love their wives as their own bodies. He that loveth his wife loveth himself. For no man ever yet hated his own flesh; but nourisheth and cherisheth it, even as the Lord the church: For we are members of his body, of his flesh, and of his bones. For this cause shall a man leave his father and mother, and shall be joined unto his wife, and they two shall be one flesh.

Husbands have to love (show affection, get mushy, be kind and gentle, and make her smile) to their wives, and do all it takes to sanctify, cleanse, and lead her in truth by the word. Just as you wash yourself, preparing for presentation, do for her; that you will have a clean and holy wife, pure in her actions toward you.

Verses 32-33: This is a great mystery: but I speak concerning Christ and the church. Nevertheless let every one of you in particular so love his wife even as himself; and the wife [see] that she reverence [her] husband.

Again, we must love and submit accordingly in order to have GODs approval in marriage. This is not a setup for a lifeless union, but a setup for heaven on earth. Accept it as GOD's way or leave it alone.

Back to 1 Corinthians 7:4-5 The wife hath not power of her own body, but the husband:

and likewise also the husband hath not power of his own body, but the wife. Defraud ye not one the other, except [it be] with consent for a time, that ye may give yourselves to fasting and prayer; and come together again, that Satan tempt you not for your incontinency.

Sex is directly tied into submission here; both have to give up authority of their own body, understanding that sex belongs to the other by right. Do not refuse to have relations with one another (no more headaches, I'm tired, or we did it yesterday) all in context of course. Nevertheless, the sacrifice is doing what pleases GOD, even if you are not in the mood. This is only to help the union, because more often than not, extra marital affairs occur when someone is not getting what they need and/or want at home. The enemy always tempts through lack, which is why GOD set marriage up this way to be no lack; there is only consensual abstinence for prayer and fasting. In order to fulfill this mandate in marriage, it cannot be about you but the other.

How to overcome in marriage.

Ephesians 6:12 For we wrestle not against flesh and blood, but against principalities, against powers, against the rulers of the darkness of this world, against spiritual wickedness in high [places].

When things seem to be going bad, don't fight each other, but fight Satan together. Even JESUS said that a house divided against itself cannot stand. You cannot see victory in your home if you are mad at one another, instead of taking your frustrations out on the one causing the ruckus in your life. The same energy you use to yell at each other and stay mad for something you did not like, pool together and start some effectual fervent prayer; because, one can put a thousand to flight, but two can put ten thousand to flight. JESUS says in Matthew 18:19 Again I say unto you, That if two of you shall agree on earth as touching any thing that they shall ask, it shall be done for them of my Father which is in heaven. The two of you are an unstoppable force, when you are on one accord.

Do not point the finger, fight; do not lay down responsibility, fight; do not just sit there and let the devil beat you or your spouse up, fight; fight the good fight of faith, and let the devil know you were the wrong one to mess with.

Finally, keep your mind on CHRIST and not on the things you consider the faults or shortcomings of the other.

Isaiah 26:3 Thou wilt keep [him] in perfect peace, [whose] mind [is] stayed [on thee]: because he trusteth in thee.

PARENTING

Proverbs 22:6 Train up a child in the way he should go: and when he is old, he will not depart from it.

You as a parent must know the way to show your child the way, lead by example; you have to be living it to get them to live it. Although, as a parent you can't close the child off from everything that goes on in the world, for the sake of Christianity, as if that is what keeps sin out of your house. That way of thinking usually leads to an overwhelming hunger towards the things that were not given any guidance or understanding. You cannot keep them in the house forever. If you give your child a clear guideline of not so much what they can't do, but what they can do; they tend to like that feeling of freedom, and usually do not stray toward the wrong. Although, that is good for adolescent years, once they get a little older it is time to set up boundaries; while still not keeping them completely shielded, let them do some stuff, like movies, beach, mall, hang out with friends, sports at school, etc. Remember, an exercise in healthy freedom leads to strength and character, but when kids are kept in a box, they take freedom at any turn and fall into pits of depravity because of ignorance.

Now, I am all for discipline, if you spare the rod you spoil the child, but don't provoke your child to wrath, Ephesians 6:4. Kids have buttons just like adults, don't push them because you are the elder and command seniority; this causes rebellion in the home, which leads to overboard discipline and a separation due to lack of understanding. These kids usually become runaways and take on malicious and deviant behavior. However, through loving kindness, wisdom, and knowledge in the word, let the SPIRIT of GOD in you draw and lead them in righteousness.

If we push our children away, they will have to learn respect, brotherhood, fatherhood, and motherhood in the streets; even worse, they will try to learn religion in the streets. Instead, let us be transformed by the word, and in it teach them of this relationship with CHRIST.

It is easy to lose focus on what is more important when raising a child, we can pay more attention to the physical aspects of life and neglect the spiritual. Take into account that people say to their kids every day that they can be president, a doctor, lawyer, or any other high-end job, making lots of money; of course, we want them to succeed in life, but that is not the measure of success. It is better to teach children to measure their lives by the fruit on their tree, spiritually; let them know that pleasing GOD is more important than making money, and doing HIS will more than getting ahead in their own way. Instead, figure out their calling in GOD and push them in that direction, which is what will give them fulfillment in life anyway.

Let us teach our children to be repairers of the breach, and to prepare the way of the LORD. AMEN.

FOR THE YOUNG FOLKS

Luke 2:49 And he said unto them, how is it that ye sought me? wist ye not that I must be about my Father's business?

This was a twelve-year-old boy speaking, yes, HE is the LORD, but HE is also our example for how to live; you can do everything JESUS did, if you are willing to turn away from doing only what pleases you, and let GOD put you in that place that HE wants you to be.

What is most important at your age? What are most 12-year-old children doing these days? Probably playing video games, going to the movies, and hanging with friends; in addition to planning their next birthday party, they are not doing anything important in GOD, for the most part.

However, JESUS says something not many young people can understand, even HIS parents did not get it. While other kids are just being kids, playing in the dirt and eating junk food; just doing what is normal in the eyes of parents and society, JESUS says how could you not know what I was doing? How is this not obvious? Why did you assume I would be like everyone else? HE basically says, you should have known where I was, according to what the angel told you before I was born. This is my makeup, HE says, I can be no different; but you thought my ministry would not start until I was 20.

JESUS says I know who I am and I have made my choice. Have you?

Therefore, you do not have to wait until you are an adult to be someone special or important in CHRIST; you do not have to wait a few more years to be used by GOD in a mighty way. Your time is now.

I will use my wife's younger sister as an example. She moved in with us when she was 13, unsaved and in need of something better, living quarters and all. She received CHRIST a few months to a year later, and through the next few years, kept studying and talking to my wife and I about getting closer to GOD. She understands doing HIS will above her own, and allowing GOD to work HIS plan; she is now in the place where, at the age of 17, she has been set aside as a minister and prophetess. In addition, she has excellent grades in all a.p. classes.

All I am saying is, your age does not determine the anointing of GOD on your life, your age does not determine whether or not GOD is going to use you, your age does not determine when GOD will give you a platform to minister HIS word in some way. It could be dance, rap, preaching, teaching, prophecy, praise and worship, etc.

It is all about your willingness to do what HE says, your willingness to trust that HE knows better than you do. Something you must realize is, the closer you get to GOD and the better you get to know HIM, the better you will get to know yourself, your purpose is in CHRIST alone and no matter what you do, you will never truly be at peace or find fulfillment till you do what you were created to do.

You do not have to be the future church; you can be the church in operation today. YOUR TIME IS NOW.

Everything we strive for, all the goals we set, start with the purpose of getting prestige; we have to change that reason to, everything we do is for the glory of GOD. You can have the best of heaven now, but you have to choose.

The time is now and it starts here.

2 Corinthians 6:2 For he saith, I have heard thee in a time accepted, and in the day of salvation have I succored thee: behold, now [is] the accepted time; behold, now [is] the day of salvation.

You must receive the free gift of salvation from GOD.

Romans 10:9-10 That if thou shalt confess with thy mouth the Lord Jesus, and shalt believe in thine heart that God hath raised him from the dead, thou shalt be saved.

For with the heart man believeth unto righteousness; and with the mouth confession is made unto salvation.

And again, Luke 2:49b wist ye not that I must be about my Father's business?

You must be about the business of GOD. It is not always going to feel good or be easy to do what HE says, but it will always be worth it.

Finally, wherever you are in CHRIST, take it to the next level. There is a deeper walk in the LORD. YOUR TIME IS NOW. AMEN.

THESE SIGNS SHALL FOLLOW

Mark 16:17-18 And these signs shall follow them that believe; in my name shall they cast out devils; they shall speak with new tongues; they shall take up serpents; and if they drink any deadly thing, it shall not hurt them; they shall lay hands on the sick, and they shall recover.

When JESUS says MY name, HE means power, authority, and character; in order to use HIS power, authority, and character, we have to be believers and operating in right standing. Once we have that strait, the spirit realm talked about in Ephesians 6 will recognize us as a threat; when we speak, mountains will move; when we fight, it is not in vain; when the weapon is formed against us, it will not prosper. But, Acts 19:15 shows the outcome of not walking in the authority of JESUS, and the evil spirit said, JESUS I know, and Paul I know; but who are you? And the attacked the man, he was not even a believer.

Also, the bible is not telling us to take up serpents, just pointing out some particular things, among many, which will no longer hurt us; of course, in the context of how we are living.

1 Corinthians 12:7-11 A spiritual gift is given to each of us as a means of helping the entire church.

To one person the Spirit gives the ability to give wise advice; to another he gives the gift of special knowledge. The Spirit gives special faith to another, and to someone else he gives the power to heal the sick. He gives one person the power to perform miracles, and to another the ability to prophesy. He gives someone else the ability to know whether it is really the Spirit of God or another spirit that is speaking. Still another person is given the ability to speak in unknown languages, and another is given the ability to interpret what is being said. It is the one and only Holy Spirit who distributes these gifts. He alone decides which gift each person should have. (NLT)

All these gifts, signs, and miracles will follow those who begin to take on the characteristics of CHRIST; as we realize the context and reason for what we do as Christians, we will begin to see that deeper walk in the LORD showing forth in our lives.

Moreover, once you allow GOD to assimilate the information in this book to wisdom, you will have no choice but to WALK IN AUTHORITY.

Now, go study the book of acts, and take it to the streets. GOD BLESS.

Printed in the United States
204849BV00003B/208-309/P

9 781603 831079